WHAT DO YOU KNOW ABOUT
ROCKS
AND FOSSILS?

ANNA CLAYBOURNE

PowerKiDS
press

Published in 2018 by **The Rosen Publishing Group, Inc.**
29 East 21st Street, New York, NY 10010

CATALOGING-IN-PUBLICATION DATA
Names: Claybourne, Anna.
Title: What do you know about rocks and fossils? / Anna Claybourne.
Description: New York : PowerKids Press, 2018. | Series: Test your science skills | Includes index.
Identifiers: ISBN 9781538323120 (pbk.) | ISBN 9781538322178 (library bound) | ISBN 9781538323137 (6 pack)
Subjects: LCSH: Rocks--Juvenile literature. | Minerals--Juvenile literature. | Fossils--Juvenile literature.
Classification: LCC QE432.2 C627 2018 | DDC 552--dc23

Copyright © 2018 Franklin Watts, a division of Hachette Children's Group

Series Editor: Amy Pimperton
Series Designer: Emma DeBanks
Picture Researcher: Diana Morris

Picture credits: Arctic –Images/Getty Images: 20cl. Roman Babakin/Shutterstock: 15br. Anna Baldwin/Shutterstock: 3br. Beboy/Shutterstock: 5cr. Ocskay Bence/Shutterstock: 4b. Bildagentur Zoonar GmbH/Shutterstock: 10t. Philippe Bourseiller/Getty Images: 6bl. Richard Bowden/Shutterstock: 8tr. Tyler Boyes/Shutterstock: 4c, 8c. Sumit Buranarothtrakul/Shutterstock: 6tl. Leonello Calvetti/Dreamstime: 4tr. Marcel Clemens/Shutterstock: 8br, 29b.Paul Crash/Shutterstock: 3bc. Dailin/Shutterstock: 16c. Henning Dalhoff/SPL: 20c. Designua/Shutterstock: 22c. fivespots/ Shutterstock: 14br. Flashgun/Shutterstock: 9t. George Photo CM/Shutterstock: 14c. Givaga/Shutterstock: 15bl. Simon Gurney/Dreamstime: 5cl. Mark Higgins/Dreamstime: 25b. Ivaylo Ivanov/Shutterstock: 19t. Jakinnboaz/Shutterstock: 22b. Jakub Janele/Shutterstock: 18b. jencon/istockphoto: 13c. Sakdinon Kadchiangsaen/Shutterstock: 8bl. Luka Kikina/ Shutterstock: 23b. Ted Kinsman/SPL: 23c. Kiril l/Shutterstock: 10c. Jonathan Lesange/Getty Images: front cover. Alex Lukin/Shutterstock: 8tcb. Marafona/Shutterstock: 1. Melba Photo Agency/Alamy: 11t, 29t. Melica/Shutterstock: 12t. Mopic/Shutterstock: 20t. NationalParks/wikimedia commons CC-BT-SA-2.5: 16br. N-2-s/Shutterstock: 10b. Yoshiaki Nagashima/Pacific Press Service/Alamy: 22t. Ken Niphon/Shutterstock: 14t. paleontologist natural/Shutterstock: 6bc. Maxim Petrichuk/Shutterstock: 16cl. Pixeljoy/Shutterstock: 24c. Anastasia Polonets/Dreamstime: 27br. Mong Pro/Shutterstock: 8bc. Pung/Shutterstock: 4cr. randy andy/Shutterstock: 18t. Alexander Raths/Shutterstock: 25t. Jane Rix/Shutterstock: 16b. David Roland/Shutterstock: 26bc. Albert Russ/Shutterstock: 12br. www.sandatlas.org/ Shutterstock: 8cr. Vladimir Sazonov//Shutterstock: 24t. Science Stock Photography/SPL: 14b. Sementer/Shutterstock: 5b. shipfactory/Shutterstock: 21tr. Andrei Shumskiy/Shutterstock: 7r. Sigur/Shutterstock: 8tc. Peter Stein/Shutterstock: 16cr. Paul D Stewart/SPL: 26br. Kuttelvaserova Stuchelova/Shutterstock: 16tb. Alison R Taylor (University of North Carolina Wilmington Microscopy Facility)/CC Wikimedia Commons 2.5: 19b. Steven J Taylor/Shutterstock: 17t. timquo/Shutterstock: 21tl. T W van Urk/Shutterstock: 11b. Jiri Vaclavek/Shutterstock: 7b, 13b. VDP/Shutterstock: 11c. Vicktor l/Shutterstock: 12bc. Steve Vidler/Alamy: 26t. S Vladislav /Shutterstock: 8cl. Krailurk Warasup/Shutterstock: 15bc. Wikimedia Commons: 20bc, 32b. Wildnerdpix/Shutterstock: 16t. Woe/Shutterstock: 4tl. xpixel/Shutterstock: 11cb. Mahathir Mohd Yasin/Shutterstock: 23t. Yurok/Shutterstock: 6tr. Frank Zack/Shutterstock: 26c. Zelenskaya/ Shutterstock: 5t. Andrii Zhezhera/Shutterstock: 17b. Zzvet/Shutterstock: 20cr.

Every attempt has been made to clear copyright. Should there be any inadvertent omission please apply to the publisher for rectification.

Manufactured in China
CPSIA Compliance Information: Batch BW18PK. For Further Information contact Rosen Publishing, New York, New York at 1-800-237-9932.

CONTENTS

Worlds in **bold** can be found in the glossary on page 30.

A note about measurements
Measurements are given in U.S. form with
metric in parentheses. The metric conversion
is rounded to make it easier to measure.

ROCKS, MINERALS, AND FOSSILS

Rock is the natural substance that the Earth is made of. On the Earth's surface, or **crust**, rocks are mostly solid and hard. The inside of the Earth is very hot at around 7,200 °F (4,000 °C), and the rock here — called the **mantle** — is partly melted.

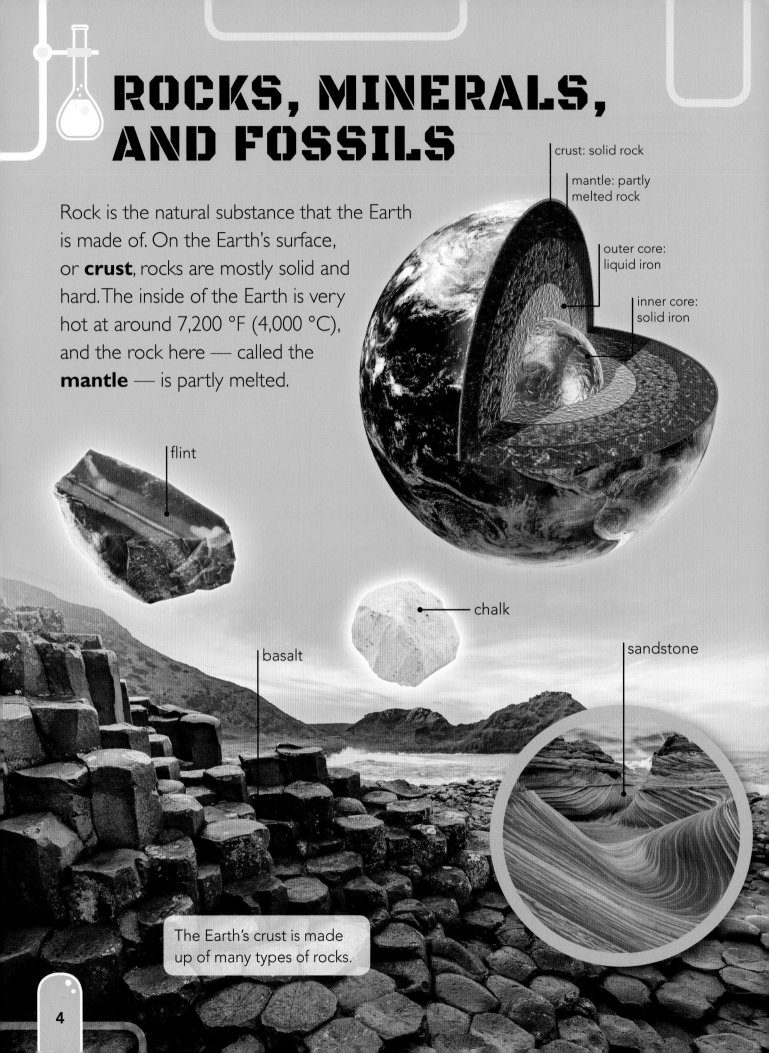

crust: solid rock

mantle: partly melted rock

outer core: liquid iron

inner core: solid iron

flint

chalk

basalt

sandstone

The Earth's crust is made up of many types of rocks.

MINERALS

Rocks are made up of **minerals**. Some rocks only contain one mineral. Others contain mixtures of minerals. A mineral is a pure, natural substance from the ground. This means it's the same all the way through — it's not a mixture of different things. Minerals include some metals, such as iron and gold, and gemstones, such as diamonds and quartz.

Granite is a rock made up of a mixture of minerals, including quartz, feldspar, and mica.

THE ROCK CYCLE

- Rivers and seas wear down rocks, creating valleys and coastal cliffs.
  - Old rocks wear down, crack apart and break up into sand, dust, and **silt**.
    - New rocks form from sand and mud on the seabed.
    - Volcanoes throw out **lava** (melted rock), which hardens to make new rock.
  - Earthquakes crush, move, and crack rocks.

This process of rocks breaking down and forming again is called the rock cycle.

A rock, stone, or pebble might seem like a very hard, long-lasting object that doesn't change much. But over long periods of time, Earth's rocks change a *lot*.

ROCKS AND HUMANS

Rocks are incredibly important to humans. Besides living our whole lives on the Earth's rocky crust, we dig up all kinds of rocks and minerals to make many of the things we need.

FINDING FOSSILS

Rocks also hold a record of life in the past in the form of **fossils**. Fossils are made when rocks form around the remains or imprints of living things. Over time, the animal or plant material is replaced by rocks and minerals, but the shape of the creature can still be seen.

This is a fossilized trilobite, a type of animal that lived from around 520 million to 250 million years ago.

THE SCIENCE OF ROCKS AND FOSSILS

Besides using rocks, we also study them to try to find out more about them. This is the science of rocks. The word "science" simply means "knowledge" — so science means trying to learn about things and understand them.

There are many branches of science to do with rocks, minerals, and fossils. Together they are known as the Earth sciences. Studying and understanding these things helps us in all kinds of ways.

Geology is the science of rocks and the way they form the Earth. Studying them reveals how the Earth has changed over time to become what it is now. It also helps us to figure out where useful rocks and minerals can be found.

Mineralogy is the study of minerals and how they can be used.

Volcanology is the science of volcanoes, and **seismology** is the science of earthquakes. By studying them and how they work, scientists can often predict volcanic eruptions, earthquakes, and landslides, and help to save lives.

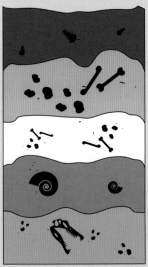

newest rocks contain the youngest fossils

time

oldest rocks contain the oldest fossils

Palaeontology (*pay-lee-on-tol-ogy*) is the study of fossils, which helps us to understand the history of life on Earth.

WORKING SCIENTIFICALLY

This book contains experiments and investigations that will help you find out more about rocks and fossils.

To do experiments, scientists use careful, logical methods to make sure they get reliable results. The experiments in this book use four key scientific methods, along with an easy acronym to help you remember them: **ATOM**.

 ## ASK

What do you want to find out?

Asking questions is an important part of science. Scientists think about what questions they have, and how to find answers.

 ## TEST

Setting up an experiment that will test ideas and answer questions

Scientists design experiments to answer questions. Tests work best if you only test for one thing at a time.

 ## OBSERVE

Key things to look out for

Scientists watch their experiments closely to see what is happening.

 ## MEASURE

Measuring and recording results, such as temperatures, sizes or amounts of time

Making accurate measurements and recording the results shows what the experiment has revealed.

WHAT NEXT?

After each experiment, the What Next? section gives you ideas for further activities and experiments, or ways to display your results.

TYPES OF ROCKS

Geologists divide rocks into three types, depending on how they form.

shale

limestone

SEDIMENTARY ROCKS

Sedimentary rocks form as rocky grains of sand or mud collect in layers. Over time, the **sediment** is pressed down by the layers on top, and gets harder.

sandstone

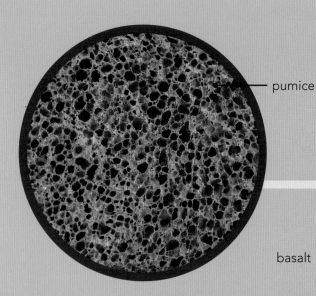

pumice

IGNEOUS ROCKS

The word **igneous** means "fiery." Igneous rocks form when hot, melted rock, such as **magma** or lava from a volcano, cools and hardens.

basalt

obsidian

METAMORPHIC ROCKS

The word "metamorphosis" means "transformation." **Metamorphic** rocks form when other rocks are heated or squeezed underground.

lapis lazuli

marble

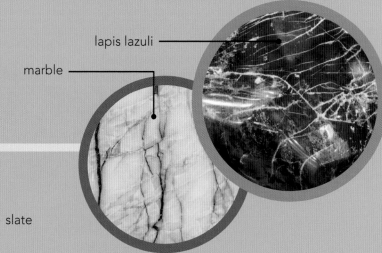

slate

Ask an adult to supervise you while using hot tap water and the knife.

YOU WILL NEED:

2 large bars of chocolate
I dark, I white
• Grater • 2 plates
• 2 small bowls • Hot water
• Plasic wrap • Spoon
• Butter knife
• Thermometer (optional)

SCIENCE EXPERIMENT:

CHOC ROCKS

A great way to see how the three rock types form is to make a model out of chocolate.

Melted chocolate forms a thick, sticky liquid, just like melted rock does.

 ## Ask

How are different types of rock made?

 ## Test

• Wash and dry your hands.
• Grate the white and dark chocolate onto separate plates. This is easier if the chocolate is cold.
• Line the small bowl with a large piece of plastic wrap so that it hangs over the sides.
• Spoon a very thin layer of grated dark chocolate into the bowl, then a very thin layer of grated white chocolate. Repeat until the bowl is full.
• Wrap the plastic wrap over the top, then push down hard on the chocolate layers to squeeze them into a solid block again.
• Unwrap it and cut a piece off. You've made sedimentary chocolate rock!

• Wrap up the rest again. This time squeeze and press it with your hands for a few minutes.
• Unwrap it and cut a piece off. This is a metamorphic chocolate rock!
• Wrap the rest up again tightly. Run hot tap water into the bowl. Put the wrapped chocolate in the water until it melts. Unwrap it, pour it into the other bowl and leave it to cool. It's an igneous chocolate rock!

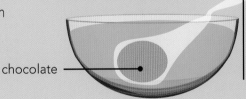

chocolate

plastic wrap

 ## Observe

Do the three rock types look different? Look at the pictures of rocks on page 8. Can you see any similarities?

 ## Measure

How hot does water have to be to melt chocolate? Find out using a thermometer, if you have one.

WHAT NEXT?

Can you find out the temperatures that rocks melt at? (It's a lot hotter than chocolate!)

ROCKS AND WATER

Did you know that some rocks can soak up water, while others can't do this at all?

POROUS AND NONPOROUS

Porous rocks have tiny spaces in them, which water can soak into. For example, sandstone is a porous rock. It is made up of rounded grains of rock that have small gaps between them, even when they are tightly packed together.

Granite (see page 5) is a type of **nonporous** rock. It is made with **interlocking** grains with hardly any spaces between them, so water cannot soak in easily.

Tiny sand grains (like the ones shown magnified above) are rounded because they are worn smooth through **friction**, but when the grains are pressed into sandstone (below), the rock has a rough, crumbly texture.

UNDERGROUND WATER

Some types of porous rock, such as sandstone, are very useful. They can store water under the ground — called **groundwater** — when it rains. The very top of the layer of groundwater is called the **water table**.

People can then dig wells to reach the water and pump it out to use it. Often groundwater finds its own way back to the surface through porous rocks, where it **emerges** as a **spring**.

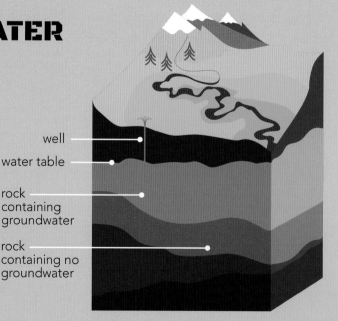

well

water table

rock containing groundwater

rock containing no groundwater

SCIENCE EXPERIMENT:
WET ROCK TEST

It's hard to see the little spaces inside most rocks. But you can test which rocks are porous using a scale.

YOU WILL NEED:

- Selection of pebbles or pieces of rock, such as chalk, quartz, amber, and slate
- Digital scale used for baking
- Bowl • Water • Paper towel
- Paper and pencil

ASK

Which rocks can hold water and which rocks can't?

Scientists use microscopes to see the holes in some rocks. This piece of basalt has been magnified many times so the (black) holes can be seen.

TEST

- Weigh your rocks in grams and write down the weight of each one. If you don't know the type of rock, describe or draw it.
- Put all of your rocks into a bowl of water and leave them there for 10 minutes.
- Take the rocks out and dry them on a paper towel so there is no water on the surface.
- Now weigh all the rocks again.

OBSERVE

Which rocks are heavier after being soaked? Which weigh the same as before? If they are heavier, it means they are holding water.

WHAT NEXT?

Make a chart that arranges your rocks in order according to how much water they can hold. Can you find out the names of some other porous rocks?

MEASURE

How much heavier did the porous rocks get compared to before they got wet? Can you work out the increase in weight as a percentage?

Slate is a type of rock used to make roof tiles. Do you think slate is porous or nonporous? (Answer on page 32.)

11

MINERALS AND CRYSTALS

A mineral, such as gold, salt, or quartz, is made of the same material all the way through. Unlike many rocks, it is not a mixture of different things.

salt

This means that a mineral, such as salt, only contains one type of **molecule**. Molecules are the tiny units that all **matter**, or stuff, is made of. They are made up of even smaller parts called **atoms**. Both are much too small to see normally, but they can be shown in diagrams like these:

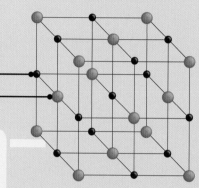

sodium atom

chloride atom

This diagram shows how atoms are bonded together to make salt molecules.

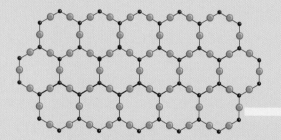

This molecule diagram shows the mineral quartz.

CRYSTAL SHAPES

Minerals often grow gradually as the molecules they are made of join together. If there is plenty of space around them, they can sometimes form a **crystal**. This is a **geometric** shape, such as a hexagon or a cube, formed by the way the molecules in the mineral fit together.

Salt and quartz (right) can both form crystals.

YOU WILL NEED:

- Table salt
- Hot water
- A jar
- Spoon • String • Scissors
- Ruler • Paper clip • Pencil
- Magnifying glass
- Food coloring

SCIENCE EXPERIMENT:

GROW SALT CRYSTALS

The salt we put in our food is a mineral also known as halite. You can use it to grow your own mineral crystals.

 ## Ask

How can you help salt crystals to form?

 ## Test

- Fill the jar about half way with hot tap water.
- Add a spoonful of salt and stir well until it dissolves and disappears.
- Keep adding salt and stirring until no more will dissolve and some salt is left at the bottom.
- Cut a piece of string about 8 inches (20 cm) long. Tie one end around the pencil and the other end to the paper clip.
- Lie the pencil across the neck of the jar so that the string and paper clip dangle in the water.
- Leave in a safe place, such as a cupboard, for a few days.

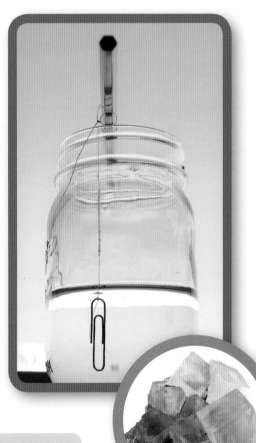

 ## Observe

Each day, check to see what is happening. Are crystals growing on the string?

Can you see any cube-shaped crystals like these?

 ## Measure

How big are the biggest crystals? Have any of them grown in geometric shapes?

WHAT NEXT?

If you have a magnifying glass or a microscope, use it to look closely at your crystals.

Try doing the experiment again, but this time add food coloring to the mixture. Does this make colored crystals?

HOW HARD?

Rocks have many different features called **properties**. For example, is a rock porous or nonporous? What color is it? Is it transparent or **opaque**, shiny or dull? Properties like these decide what each type of rock can be used for.

Hardness is an especially important property. It decides whether a rock can be used for building, and how easy it is to cut or grind up.

Granite is a very hard rock. It's used to make kitchen counters and tools.

Mica, a soft, shiny mineral, is crushed and used to make glittery makeup.

A granite pestle and mortar is used for grinding hard seeds.

THE MOHS SCALE

To indicate how hard a rock is, geologists use a scale called the **Mohs scale of hardness**, which was invented by German scientist Friedrich Mohs (1773–1839).

1 talc   2 gypsum   3 calcite   4 fluorite   5 apatite

6 feldspar   7 quartz   8 topaz   9 corundum   10 diamond

The scale runs from 1 (very soft) to 10 (very hard). Each step on the scale has a typical rock or mineral of that hardness as an example.

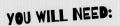

YOU WILL NEED:

- 10–20 different pebbles and rocks
- A large new steel nail
- An oven mitt
- Pencil and paper

SCIENCE EXPERIMENT:

HARD AS NAILS

This scratch test lets you sort out rocks into harder and softer types.

 ASK

How do we know which rocks are harder and which are softer?

 OBSERVE

What happens to each rock? If the nail makes a scratch in the rock, the rock is softer than the nail. But if the nail draws a silvery mark on the rock, the rock is harder than the nail.

 TEST

- Gather a selection of different pebbles and rocks. If you know the names of them, write them down. Otherwise, write down descriptions of them.
- To test each rock, hold it firmly in an oven mitt to avoid hurting yourself with the nail.
- Try to scratch the rock with the pointed end of the nail. (A nail has a rating of about 4 on the Mohs hardness scale.)

 MEASURE

Sort out your rock samples into harder and softer categories. How many are there in each group?

WHAT NEXT?

Try scratching the rocks with each other to see which is best at scratching the others. Can you arrange your rocks in order of hardness?

Why do you think many castles were built out of stone?

WEATHERING AND EROSION

Rocks are always wearing away. This happens in two stages: **weathering** and **erosion**.

Weathering happens when rock is broken into smaller and smaller pieces.

Waves hit cliffs and break off boulders, which then break into rocks, pebbles, and grains.

As they grow, tree roots can push rocks apart.

Water is gradually **dissolving** these rocks as it flows over them, creating a **gorge**.

Erosion happens when the bits of rock get carried away and moved to new places.

Sand grains are easily blown away by the wind.

Streams and rivers carry sand, pebbles, and rocks towards the sea.

SHAPING THE LAND

Weathering and erosion shape rocks into sheer cliffs, smooth pebbles, or amazing rock formations. They gradually carve valleys and wear down mountaintops.

West Mitten Butte in Monument Valley, Arizona (left) and this rock in Mushroom Rock State Park, Kansas (right) were formed when softer rock weathered and eroded faster than the harder rock, creating these interesting shapes.

YOU WILL NEED:

- A large plastic tray or a large, deep pan
- Sand
- Water
- Plastic bottle
- Small toy houses (or you can use sugar cubes or candy)
- Camera or smartphone

 SCIENCE EXPERIMENT:

SEA AND SHORE

Waves breaking on the shore weather and erode the land, shaping the coast (see right). You can make a model this using sand and water in a tray.

 ## ASK

How do waves change a coastline?

 ## OBSERVE

Watch how the waves affect the shoreline and what happens to the sand and houses.

TEST

- Add some water to your sand so that it holds together and use it to fill one end of your tray. Pack it together tightly to make a seashore. Put toy houses on the shore.
- Fill the rest of the tray with water to make the sea.
- Hold the bottle horizontal and parallel to the shore. Push it up and down in the water to make waves.

water

 ## MEASURE

Measure the position of the shoreline and houses before and after by taking photos from above.

WHAT NEXT?

Try filling the tray with sand, tilting it, then pouring a trickle of water down it from the top end. This models how flowing rivers carve and shape the land.

Sometimes houses really do fall into the sea because of coastal erosion.

EXPANDING ICE

Water **expands**, or gets bigger, as it freezes. This causes a very important type of weathering called **freeze-thaw weathering**, especially in cold, damp parts of the world. Here's how it works.

Freeze-thaw weathering can even crack big boulders in half.

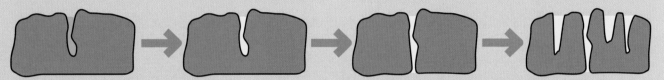

1. Liquid water soaks into a porous rock, or into cracks that have already formed in rocks.

2. In colder weather, often at night, the temperature drops and the water freezes.

3. As it expands into ice, it pushes the rock apart, making more or bigger cracks.

4. This happens over and over again, and eventually cracks rocks into small pieces.

WEATHERED WALLS

Freeze-thaw weathering doesn't just happen to natural rocks and boulders. It can also affect houses and walls built out of stone or human-made rock-like materials, such as bricks, concrete, and plaster.

This wall has been damaged by weathering.

SCIENCE EXPERIMENT:
FREEZING CHALK

Chalk is a sedimentary rock made from the crushed shells of microscopic living things called coccoliths. The shells contain calcium. The type of chalk you use to write on a chalkboard or pavement is made in a factory, but it is very similar as it also contains the same types of minerals. This experiment shows how freeze-thaw weathering works using factory-made chalk.

YOU WILL NEED:

- 2 sticks of chalk, the same size and type
- Bowl
- Water
- Freezer
- Two small plastic food bags
- A chalkboard or pavement

ASK

What happens to chalk (a porous rock) when it gets wet, then freezes?

TEST

- First, try drawing with both chalk sticks on the chalkboard or pavement to check they are both firm and strong.
- Fill the bowl with water and put one of the sticks of chalk in. Let it soak for 10 minutes.
- Now put the wet chalk in one plastic bag and the dry chalk in the other.
- Put both bags in the freezer and leave them to freeze overnight.
- Take the bags out and take the sticks of chalk out of the bags.
- Try drawing with the chalks again.

OBSERVE

Look for differences between the two sticks of chalk.

MEASURE

How long does each stick last when you try to use it after it has been in the freezer?

WHAT NEXT?

If you can't see a clear difference between your two chalk sticks, try repeating the experiment again.

When you're out and about in the countryside or city, look out for weathered stone to see how it has broken apart.

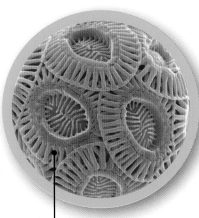

a magnified ball of coccoliths

MAKING MOUNTAINS

The Earth is covered in a crust of hard rock — but this crust is not all in one piece.

Instead, it's made up of huge sections called **tectonic plates**. They fit together like puzzle pieces. All the time, the plates are slowly, gradually moving around.

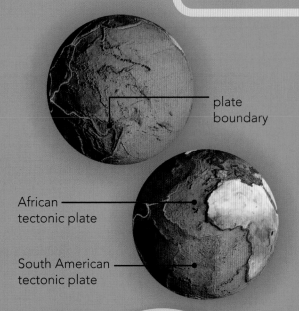

plate boundary

African tectonic plate

South American tectonic plate

Mid-Atlantic Ridge, Iceland

In some places, two plates move away from each other, and magma from inside the Earth rises up to make new land (below) or a **rift** valley forms (above). This is called a divergent boundary.

Sometimes, two plates slide against each other in different directions. This can crack or split the ground and is called a transform boundary.

San Andreas Fault, California, USA.

Himalayas, Asia

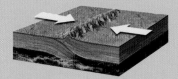

And in some places, one plate slides under another. This can make the land crumple and rise up, forming mountains. This is called a convergent boundary.

HOW SLOW?

The plates usually move so slowly, we can't see or feel it happening. For example, the Indian plate is pushing under the Eurasian plate, making the Himalayas rise higher and higher. But the plate only moves at about 2 inches (5 cm) per year — about twice as fast as your toenails grow. Meanwhile, weathering and erosion wear the mountains down.

- Modeling clay in two colors
  - Ruler or tape measure
    - Pen and paper

 SCIENCE EXPERIMENT:

PLASTICINE PLATES

Use different colors of modeling clay to make model tectonic plates and see what happens when they move around.

ASK

How do fold mountains form?

Mountains made by converging plates are sometimes called fold mountains. From the sky, they look like a folded or crumpled cloth.

TEST

- Make two flat tectonic plates in different colors out of modeling clay, about 5 inch thick (I cm).
- Lay them flat on a table so that the edges fit together.
- Then slowly push them together at the edges in the direction of the arrows so that one moves under the other, forcing it up into a model of a mountain range.

OBSERVE

Watch how the mountains grow upwards as the plates move.

WHAT NEXT?

Make two plates with a zig-zag boundary, like this.

zig-zag boundary

MEASURE

Measure the height of your mountains above the flat part of the plates. How much force do you need to apply to push them together?

Then slide them against each other in opposite directions (the direction of the arrows). Can you see cracks forming between them?

VOLCANOES AND EARTHQUAKES

Mostly, the Earth's rocky plates move slowly. But sometimes, they grind against each other and get stuck. The pressure builds up and up until the plates suddenly slip. This makes them move fast and shake, causing an earthquake.

An earthquake in Kobe, Japan, in 1995 caused a lot of damage and killed over 6,000 people.

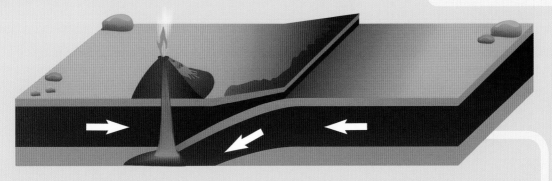

Along the edges, tectonic plates can have weak points or cracks in them. Magma from inside the Earth can push up and break through the crust, forming a volcano.

This diagram shows a volcano close to a convergent plate boundary.

INSIDE A VOLCANO

A volcano has a hole, or **vent**, leading to a **magma chamber** — an area of hot melted rock below the crust. When a volcano erupts, magma bursts out of the vent. Once it's out in the open, it's called lava. It flows out and cools, making new igneous rock. Over many eruptions, the cooled lava builds up into a mountain.

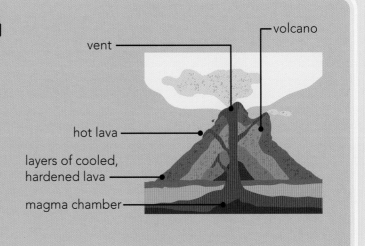

vent

volcano

hot lava

layers of cooled, hardened lava

magma chamber

ERUPTING VOLCANO

This working model of a volcano shows how the lava erupts out of the top of a volcano and flows down the sides.

red food coloring

YOU WILL NEED:

- Modeling clay
- Large tray
- A small, narrow jar or container
- White vinegar
- Red food coloring
- Baking soda
- Teaspoon
- Stopwatch
- Measuring tape or ruler

ASK

Where does lava go when a volcano erupts?

TEST

- Put the jar or container in the middle of the tray, and build a modeling clay volcano around it about 6 inches (15 cm) high. Leave an opening at the top that leads into the container.
- Add a teaspoon of baking soda to the container along with a few drops of red food coloring.
- Slowly pour the vinegar into the container to make the model volcano erupt.

* To build a really big model volcano, like the one above, make the volcano out of paper-mache, and experiment with a bigger container, more baking soda, and more vinegar!

OBSERVE

Watch how the lava flows down the sides and pools around the volcano — real lava flows like this too.

MEASURE

Measure how far away from the volcano the lava flows reach. Use a stopwatch to time how long your volcanic eruption lasts.

WHAT NEXT?

Many people live near volcanoes. Can you find out about places around the world where people live near an **active** volcano? How far away is the nearest active volcano from where you live?

Karymsky is an active volcano in Russia.

HOW FOSSILS FORM

Fossils are shapes left in rock by living things that died a long time ago.

Ammonites are one of the most common fossils you can find. These **prehistoric** sea creatures were similar to a squid, but had a snail-like shell. Larger animals, such as dinosaurs, can form fossils too. These pictures show one of the most common ways for a fossil to form.

This cluster of ammonites has been fossilized in sandstone.

This belemnite (a sea creature that was also similar to a squid) is fossilized in limestone.

1. A dinosaur dies and sinks to the bottom of a lake or sea.

2. Slowly, layers of mud and sand collect on top of the dinosaur and eventually form sedimentary rock. The soft parts of the dinosaur's body rot away.

Water in the rock flows around the bones, slowly dissolving them. Minerals in the water gradually replace the bones to form fossils.

3. Over thousands of years, weathering and erosion wear away the sedimentary rock and the fossils are exposed.

YOU WILL NEED:

- Seashells
- Modeling clay • Shallow dish
- Newspaper • Water
- Plaster • Rubber gloves
- A popsicle stick or old spoon
- An empty, clean yogurt cup

SCIENCE EXPERIMENT:
INSTANT FOSSIL

In this experiment you can make your own instant "fossils." They don't form in quite the same way as the fossils on page 24, but they show how the shape of an object can be preserved. This is how trace fossils form.

 ASK

How can the shape of a living thing become preserved in rock?

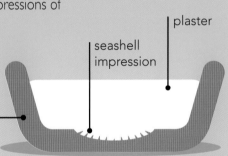

seashells

 TEST

- First, press a hand-sized piece of modeling clay into the bottom and up the sides of a shallow dish.
- Press your seashells into the middle of the modeling clay to make impressions of their shapes. Remove the objects and remove the clay from the dish.
- Put on the rubber gloves and spread newspaper on the table. In the yogurt cup, mix up some plaster with water, following the instructions on the packet.
- Fill the dish shape with the plaster mix and leave it until it is completely hard.
- Carefully peel off the modeling clay.

plaster

seashell impression

modeling clay formed into a dish shape

 OBSERVE

Can you see "fossils" in the plaster shape you have made?

MEASURE

Compare your original seashells and their "fossils" — are they the exact same size and shape?

WHAT NEXT?

Can you make "fossils" of a leaf, a handprint, or a tooth that's fallen out?

This footprint is a real trace fossil made by a dinosaur walking across soft, sandy ground millions of years ago. Over time, the ground hardened, which preserved the footprint.

FOSSIL PUZZLES

Some fossils are complete when they are found. They show a whole creature, preserved in a single piece of rock, like this starfish fossil (right).

But others, especially large fossils of big dinosaurs, are often found in pieces. The bones or other parts of the skeleton may each be fossilized separately and jumbled up in the ground.

This whole starfish was perfectly fossilized in rock.

PIECE BY PIECE

Fossil scientists, or palaeontologists, have to piece the parts together to work out how the creature looked when it was alive. To help them do this, they use their knowledge about other animals and their body shapes.

A jumble of fossilized bones is called a bonebed.

NOSE OR THUMB?

Sometimes it takes a while to get it right. When scientists discovered the dinosaur *Iguanodon*, they found a spike-shaped bone and decided it should go on the dinosaur's nose. Later, they found skeletons with two spikes and realized they belonged on its thumbs instead.

thumb spike

This drawing shows an *Iguanodon's* thumb spike.

SCIENCE EXPERIMENT:

BUILD A PREHISTORIC CREATURE

Imagine you're a paleontologist who's found a mixed-up prehistoric skeleton. Can you put the bones together to show how the animal would have looked?

 ## Ask

How do modern animals give us clues about how prehistoric creatures looked?

 ## Test

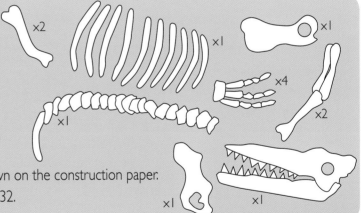

- Copy each of these groups of fossil bones the number of times indicated, then cut them out.
- Put them on your paper and try to arrange them into an animal shape.
- To help you, look at the whale skeleton shown below. It may give you some helpful clues.
- Once you're happy with it, glue the bones down on the construction paper.
- Check your result against the picture on page 32.

 ## Observe

Look at how different animals share a similar basic body "map." This reveals how living things are related to each other, even those that have died out.

 ## Measure

Which has more bones, the puzzle fossil or a human?

WHAT NEXT?

Research on the Internet to find more skeletons of prehistoric creatures. Can you find out which types of rock are best for finding fossils in?

This is the skeleton of a blue whale. This animal's body plan can help you make a "map" for the jumble of bones in the test above.

READING YOUR RESULTS

When scientists do experiments, they get results. Even if nothing happened as they expected, that is a result too! All results can be useful, but it is important to understand them. Here are some guidelines that scientists use to learn from their results.

USE A CONTROL

In experiments that test for something, scientists use a control — a normal version of the setup, without the thing that is being tested. The Freezing Chalk experiment on page 19, for example, uses two sticks of chalk.
One is soaked in water before freezing, and another, the control, is not.

It's really important that apart from the thing being tested, the control version matches the test version in every way. So the two sticks of chalk must be exactly the same, and must be treated the same way — both placed in the same type of plastic bag and kept in the same freezer for the same amount of time. Then you know that any differences in your results are purely down to the one thing that was different — in this case, the water.

REPEAT AND VERIFY

An experiment may work well once, but what if that was a fluke? So that they can be really sure of their results, scientists often repeat an experiment several times.

CHECK FOR BIAS

If you're hoping for an exciting result from your experiment, it's possible you might accidentally-on-purpose "help" your experiment along by ignoring something that doesn't fit with what you wanted. This is called "bias," and it can happen without you even realizing it. Scientists have to try to be careful to avoid bias.

OUTLIERS

What if you were conducting the Wet Rock Test experiment on page 11, and one of the rocks weighed *less* after being soaked in water? That would be very unusual and unexpected, as it would mean some of the rock had disappeared.

An unusual result like this is called an outlier. Scientists have to check outliers carefully and work out why they have happened. For example, you might have made a mistake and measured the weight incorrectly the first time. Or perhaps you've tested an unusual type of rock that dissolves very fast in water. To be sure, you might have to repeat your experiment or do some different tests.

KEEPING RECORDS

Writing down the details of each experiment and what the results were is essential for scientists. It helps them explain their work to others and look for patterns. For example, you might notice that rocks hold more or less water when the water is at different temperatures.

MAKING MISTAKES

If you spot a mistake, start the experiment again. It would be an even bigger mistake to use the results from a badly run experiment.

However, if a mistake makes something interesting happen, you could set up a new experiment to test for that instead. Many important discoveries have been made this way. For example, scientist Henri Becquerel (1852–1908) discovered **radioactivity** after leaving some uranium rocks in a drawer and noticing that they affected light-sensitive photographic plates nearby. This showed the rock was releasing some kind of energy.

GLOSSARY

active In this instance, active relates to a volcano that has erupted in the last 10,000 years.

atoms Tiny ball-like parts that all matter is made from.

chloride The chemical chlorine that has been combined with at least one other element.

crust The layer of solid rock that makes up the Earth's surface.

crystal A mineral that has formed in a regular shape, such as a cube.

dissolve To become broken down into tiny bits in a liquid.

emerge To move out of or away from something.

erosion The process that carries away rocks that have been weathered.

expand To get bigger.

fossil The shape or imprint of something that was once alive, preserved in rock.

freeze-thaw weathering A process that cracks rocks apart when water gets into them and freezes.

friction The resistance felt when one surface rubs or scrapes over another.

geology The science of rocks.

geometric A shape made up of regular lines, angles and shapes, for example a cube.

gorge A narrow valley with steep, rocky walls, usually with a stream or river running along the bottom.

groundwater Water stored in rocks or soil underground

igneous A type of rock made when melted rock from volcanoes cools and hardens.

interlocking When two things perfectly lock or join together, for example the pieces of a jigsaw.

lava Melted rock that has come out of a volcano.

magma Melted or partly melted rock inside the Earth.

magma chamber An area of magma just under the Earth's crust, which can escape when a volcano erupts.

mantle The part of Earth, between the crust and the core, which is made of melted, or partly melted rock.

matter The stuff or materials that all the things around us are made from.

metamorphic A type of rock formed when other rocks are heated or squeezed very hard underground.

mineral A natural substance found in the Earth that is pure, or the same all the way through, and not a mixture of things.

mineralogy The study of minerals.

Mohs scale of hardness A scale used to identify how hard a particular type or sample of rock is.

molecule The smallest unit that a particular type of matter can be made from. Molecules are made of atoms.

nonporous Not containing any spaces that water or other substances can soak into.

opaque Something that can't be seen through.

palaeontology The study of fossils.

porous Containing spaces that water or other substances can soak into.

prehistoric From the time before history began to be written down.

properties The features or abilities of a particular type of rock or other material.

radioactivity A type of invisible energy released by some rocks and minerals.

rift A crack, split, or break in something.

sediment Matter, such as mud, sand, or silt that settles at the bottom of a liquid.

seismology The study of earthquakes.

silt A muddy substance made of fine bits of sand or clay.

sodium A silver-white metallic chemical element.

spring A place where water wells up from underground.

tectonic plates The huge sections that make up the Earth's crust.

trace fossil A fossil that is formed from something a living thing leaves behind, such as a footprint, an egg, or a burrow.

vent An opening in the Earth's crust where magma from inside the Earth can escape.

volcanology The study of volcanoes.

water table The upper level of an underground store of groundwater.

weathering A process that wears rock down or breaks it into smaller pieces.

BOOKS

Watcher Guide: Rocks, Minerals and Gems by John Farndon, QED, 2016

Explore Fossils! With 25 Great Projects by Cynthia Light Brown and Grace Brown, Nomad Press, 2016

Everything Rocks and Minerals by Steve Tomecek, National Geographic, 2011

All About Earth: Exploring the Planet with Science Projects by Sara L. Latta, Raintree, 2016

WEBSITES

PowerKids Press has developed an online list of websites related to the subject of this book. This site is updated regularly. Please use this link to access the list:

www.powerkidslinks.com/tyss/rocks

INDEX

ANSWERS

P.11. WET ROCK TEST:
Slate is usually nonporous or has very low porosity. This is why it makes such a good material to cover roofs, as rainwater will run off the tiles rather than soaking through the rock and making the inside of the building wet.

P.27. BUILD A PREHISTORIC CREATURE:
The jumbled bones are those of the animal *Ambulocetus*, an ancestor of today's whales and hippos. The body plan should look like this picture (right).

What similarities can you see between *Ambulocetus's* skeleton and the blue whale skeleton on page 27?

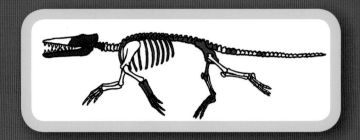